WORLD EXPLORERS

EXPEDITIONS IN THE AMERICAS

1492–1700

Stephen Currie

PICTURE AND TEXT CREDITS
Cover (back) Gianni Dagli Ort/Corbis; cover 1965.16.332: George Catlin, *La Salle's Party Entering the Mississippi in Canoes, February 6, 1682,* Paul Mellon Collection, Image © 2003 Board of Trustees, National Gallery of Art, Washington; cover (upper right), 17 Charles & Josette Lenars/Corbis; pages 1, 2, 5 (bottom left), 8 (bottom), 13 (left) Scala/Art Resource, NY; pages 3 (top), 4 (top right), 5 (bottom middle), 15 (bottom), 21 (top and bottom), 31 (top) Werner Forman/Art Resource, NY; page 3 Giraudon/Art Resource, NY; pages 4 (top left), 11 (right) Museo Nazionale Preistorico/Etnografico L. Pigorini, Rome; pages 5 (bottom right), 22–23 © Canadian Museum of Civilization, photographer Merle Toole, catalogue no. III-G-413, image no. S96-24184; pages 5 (top right), 32 Photo Researchers, Inc.; pages 6–7 Richard Schlecht/National Geographic Image Collection; page 8 (top left) Joseph Sohm; Chromosohm Inc./Corbis; pages 10, 26–27, 29 (left) Bettmann/Corbis; page 11 text from *The Broken Spears* by Miguel Leon-Portilla. Copyright © 1962 by Beacon Press. Reprinted by permission of Beacon Press; page 11 (left) PhotoDisc; page 12 Erich Lessing/Art Resource, NY; page 13 (right) National Maritime Museum; page 14 (top left) Danny Lehman/Corbis; pages 14 (bottom), 20 The Granger Collection, New York; pages 16–17, 18 Ned M. Seidler/National Geographic Image Collection; page 19 (left) Jonathan Blair/Corbis; page 19 (right) Mary Evans Picture Library; page 22 (top left) Réunion des Musées Nationaux/Art Resource, NY; page 22 (right) Corbis; page 24 1965.16.322: George Catlin, *First Sailing of the Griffon on Lake Erie, August 7, 1679,* Paul Mellon Collection, Image © 2003 Board of Trustees, National Gallery of Art, Washington; page 25 (top) 1965.16.331: George Catlin, *La Salle Crossing Lake Michigan on the Ice, December 8, 1681,* Paul Mellon Collection, Image © 2003 Board of Trustees, National Gallery of Art, Washington; page 25 (bottom) Richard T. Nowitz/Corbis; page 27 Tom Bean/Stone/Getty Images; page 28 Howard Pyle, *La Salle Petitions the King for Permission to Explore the Mississippi, Harper's Monthly,* February 1905. Courtesy of the Delaware Art Museum; page 29 (right) Robert Clark/Aurora Photos; page 30 (top left) Wolfgang Kaehler/Corbis; page 30 (right) The New York Public Library/Art Resource, NY; page 31 (bottom) © The Newberry Library/Stock Montage.

Produced through the worldwide resources of the National Geographic Society, John M. Fahey, Jr., President and Chief Executive Officer; Gilbert M. Grosvenor, Chairman of the Board; Nina D. Hoffman, Executive Vice President and President, Books and Education Publishing Group.

PREPARED BY NATIONAL GEOGRAPHIC SCHOOL PUBLISHING
Ericka Markman, Senior Vice President and President, Children's Books and Education Publishing Group; Steve Mico, Vice President, Editorial Director; Marianne Hiland, Executive Editor; Anita Schwartz, Project Editor; Jim Hiscott, Design Manager; Kristin Hanneman, Illustrations Manager; Diana Bourdrez, Picture Editor; Matt Wascavage, Manager of Publishing Services; Sean Philpotts, Production Manager.

MANUFACTURING AND QUALITY MANAGEMENT
Christopher A. Liedel, Chief Financial Officer; Phillip L. Schlosser, Director; Clifton M. Brown, Manager.

ART DIRECTION Dan Banks, Project Design Company

CONSULTANT/REVIEWER
Dr. Margit E. McGuire, School of Education, Seattle University, Seattle, Washington

BOOK DEVELOPMENT Nieman Inc.

BOOK DESIGN Three Communication Design, LLC

PICTURE EDITING AND MANAGEMENT
Corrine L. Brock/In the Lupe, Inc.

MAP DEVELOPMENT AND PRODUCTION Elizabeth Wolf

Published by the National Geographic Society
1145 17th Street, N.W.
Washington, D.C. 20036-4688

ISBN: 0-7922-4544-X

Printed in Canada

Cover: La Salle's canoes enter the Mississippi River
(top): Aztec mask
Back cover: Aztec plate
page 1: Aztec mask
page 2: Aztec funeral mask
page 3 (top): Aztec gold pendant
page 3 (bottom): Columbus arriving at San Salvador

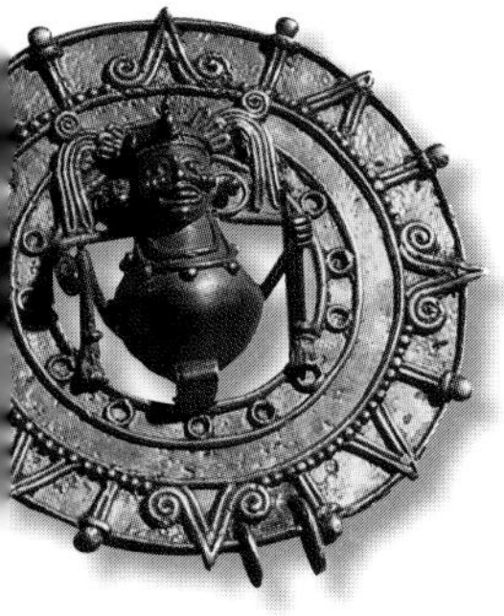

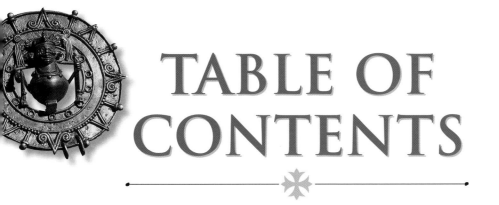

TABLE OF CONTENTS

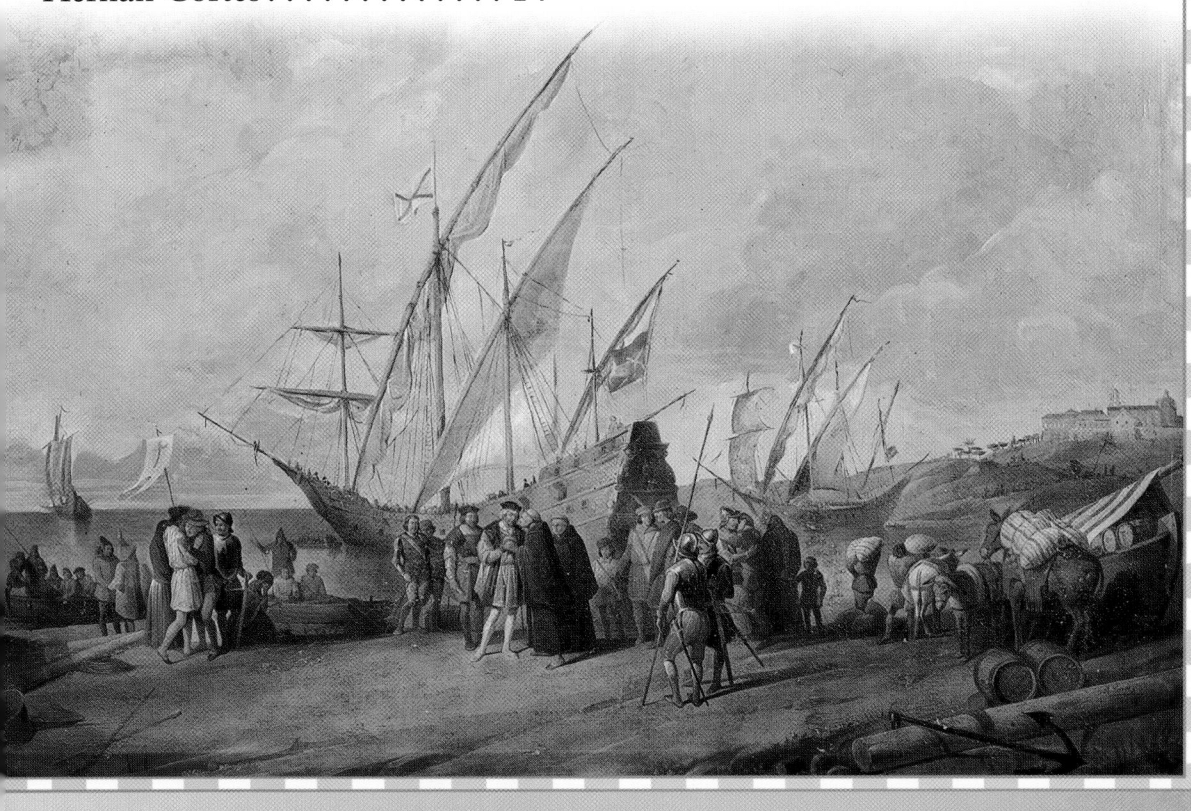

THE WORLD IN 1492

In the late 1400s, a great age of European exploration was getting into full swing. People in Europe were learning more and more about the rest of the world. They were most interested in the **Indies**, their name for the lands of eastern Asia.

These regions held great riches, such as spices, silk, jewels, and gold. People in Europe were eager to trade for these goods. Explorers from Portugal, a small country on the southwest coast of Europe, were trying to sail around Africa to reach the Indies.

◄ Aztec mask made of turquoise and pearl shell

What if there were another, shorter route to the Indies? Educated Europeans of the time knew that the world was round. So if an explorer sailed *west* from Europe, across the Atlantic Ocean, he should reach the Indies. As far as anybody knew, there was nothing in the way.

In 1492, the explorer Christopher Columbus tried sailing west across the Atlantic. He reached islands he thought were off the coast of Asia. He was wrong.

◄ The landing of Columbus on San Salvador

Columbus had reached the Western Hemisphere. During the next 200 years, the countries of Europe struggled to claim parts of this vast "New World." Between 1519 and 1521, the Spaniard Hernán Cortés conquered the Aztecs, a Native American people of Mexico. In the late 1600s, the French explorer Robert de La Salle claimed the whole Mississippi Valley for France.

Exploration of the Mississippi by de La Salle

Conquest of Mexico by Cortés

First Voyage of Columbus

| 1450 | 1500 | 1550 | 1600 | 1650 | 1700 |

CARAVELS AND CARRACKS

European explorers of the late 1400s mainly used two kinds of ships—the caravel and the carrack. The Portuguese had first developed the caravel for their voyages around Africa. The **caravel** was a small ship—no more than 75 feet (23 meters) long. It had several large, three-sided sails called **lateens**. Caravels could hold supplies for a crew of about 20 men.

The Portuguese later developed a larger version of the caravel called a **carrack**. The carrack was about 50 feet (15 meters) longer than the caravel. Because the carrack was larger, it could carry much bigger loads of supplies than the caravel. Carracks used both lateens and square sails.

The ship shown here is the *Niña*. It was the smallest of the three ships Columbus used on his first voyage to the Americas. The *Niña* was a caravel and originally had two masts for large lateen sails. Columbus later changed this. He gave the *Niña* square-rigged sails like a carrack. This allowed the ship to take better advantage of the winds. These generally blow from east to west along the route Columbus took across the Atlantic.

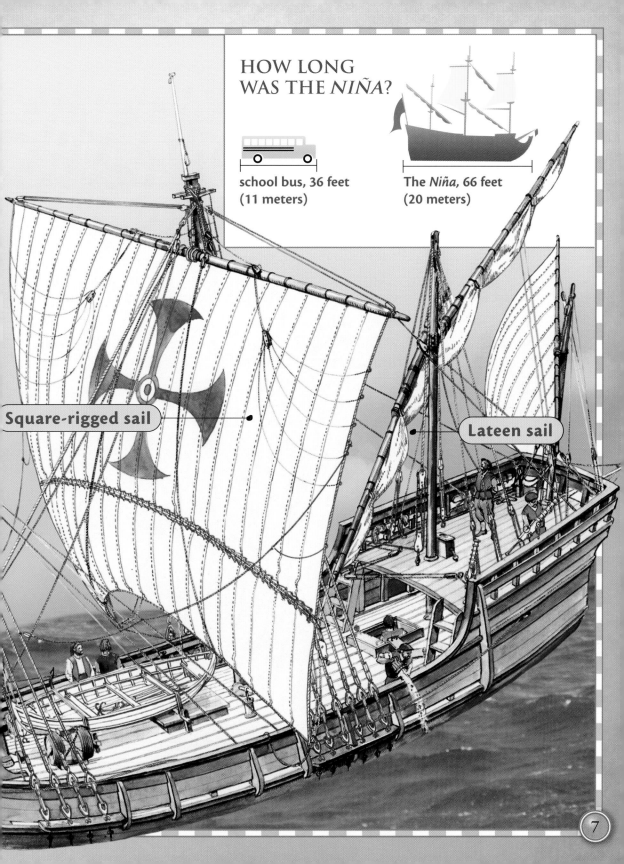

HOW LONG WAS THE *NIÑA*?

school bus, 36 feet
(11 meters)

The *Niña*, 66 feet
(20 meters)

Square-rigged sail

Lateen sail

CHAPTER 1

CHRISTOPHER COLUMBUS

Christopher Columbus was born in 1451 in Genoa, a great seaport in Italy. By the time he was 25, he was a **merchant**. Columbus made trading voyages all across the Mediterranean Sea. Later, he sailed as far north as Iceland and as far south as western Africa.

But that was not far enough for Columbus. He wanted to sail west all the way to the Indies. Many thinkers had said the voyage *should* be possible, but no one had tried yet.

Columbus vowed to be the first to make the trip. He needed someone rich enough to pay for ships, sailors, and supplies. Columbus asked King John of Portugal, but the king turned him down. Portugal was close to finding an eastern route around Africa to the Indies.

Christopher Columbus

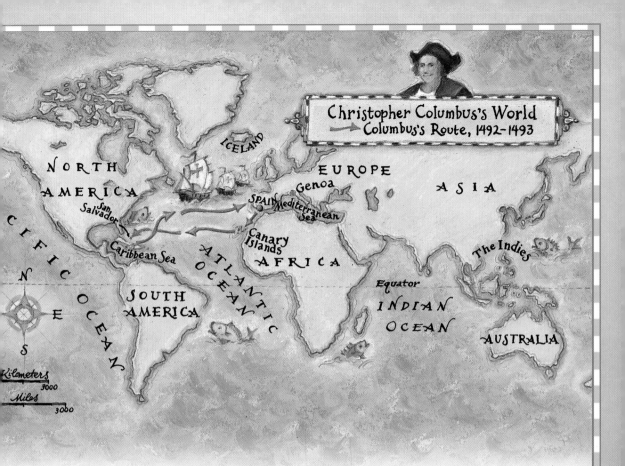

Columbus next went to King Ferdinand and Queen Isabella, the rulers of Spain. He promised to bring back great treasure for Spain. Although Ferdinand and Isabella were tempted, they weren't sure. They wondered if the Indies were *really* as close as Columbus believed. They also wondered if they could afford to give him what he needed. Finally, in the spring of 1492, they decided to support Columbus on his journey to the Indies.

On September 6, 1492, Columbus and his crew set sail in three ships from the Canary Islands, off the African coast. Already, the crewmen were fearful. Sailors of the time always stayed close to land. Columbus was planning to sail out into the middle of the open ocean. No one could tell whether the men would ever see land again.

WESTWARD TO THE INDIES

To keep the men calm, Columbus kept two **logbooks**, or records of the voyage. In his own copy, he noted how many miles he thought the ships traveled each day. Then he made a second copy for his crew, showing fewer miles traveled.

Columbus knew that the closer the men thought they were to Spain, the less fearful they would be. He did not want to face a **mutiny**, a revolt aboard ship.

Landing of Columbus on San Salvador

Day after day, the three ships sailed deeper into the unknown. The men were ready to mutiny. Finally, on October 12th, a lookout sighted land. It was an island, which Columbus named San Salvador, "Holy Savior."

The men went ashore and were greeted by the Taino (TI–noh), the Native American people who lived there. Convinced that he had reached the Indies, Columbus called the Taino "Indians." In fact, San Salvador was part of what Europeans would soon call the "New World." Asia was still thousands of miles away, but Columbus had no way of knowing that.

ACROSS CULTURES

A Taino image of a god, or zemi, made of wood, cotton, glass beads, and shell disks

Sailors used an hourglass to measure time aboard ship. Knowing how much time had passed helped them tell how far they had traveled.

Columbus wrote about the Taino in his logbook. "They are simple and generous with what they have to such a degree as no one would believe but him who had seen it. Of anything they have, if it be asked for, they never say no, but do rather invite the person to accept it, and show as much lovingness as though they would give their hearts."

Columbus reports to King Ferdinand and Queen Isabella.

RETURN TO SPAIN

During the next three months, the fleet explored other islands. The men searched for gold and claimed all the land they found for Spain. They saw none of the rich cities of Asia they expected to find. Columbus was still sure that he had reached the Indies.

Back in Spain, Columbus was hailed as a hero. He told Ferdinand and Isabella that he had been only a few miles from the richest cities in Asia. Ferdinand and Isabella were delighted to hear that Columbus had claimed so much land for Spain.

Columbus went on to make three more voyages to the Caribbean Sea and South America. He kept searching for the rich cities of Asia. Columbus was sure the next coast his ships reached would hold what he sought.

Before long, other Europeans realized that the lands Columbus had reached were not Asia at all. They were part of a "New World" unknown to Europe. Columbus refused to believe this. He died in 1506, as sure as ever that he had sailed to the Indies.

In the years after Columbus's death, many Spaniards sailed west to the lands he had found. The leaders of these voyages were called **conquistadors** (kong-KEE-stuh-dohrs), or "conquerors."

The conquistadors were part soldier and part explorer. Brave, daring, and brutal, they were eagerly searching for wealth— and for new worlds to conquer. The greatest of the conquistadors was Hernán Cortés. Cortés would find the rich cities Columbus had sought.

Ferdinand and Isabella made Columbus a nobleman. This was his family crest.

Compass used in the 1400s

13

CHAPTER 2

HERNÁN CORTÉS

Hernán Cortés was born in Spain in 1485. As a young man, he came to Cuba, one of the new lands claimed by Spain. There, Cortés heard wonderful tales of the wealth of the Aztecs.

The Aztecs were a powerful Native American people who ruled Mexico. Eager to get some of their treasure for himself, Cortés sailed to the Mexican coast in 1519. He brought with him weapons, horses, and an army of about 600 men.

Word of the Spanish arrival soon reached the Aztec emperor, Moctezuma (mok–teh–ZOO–muh). He had good reason to be curious about Cortés and his men. Quetzalcoatl (ket–sal–koh–AT–il), one of the most important Aztec gods, was said to be bearded and light-skinned.

Hernán Cortés

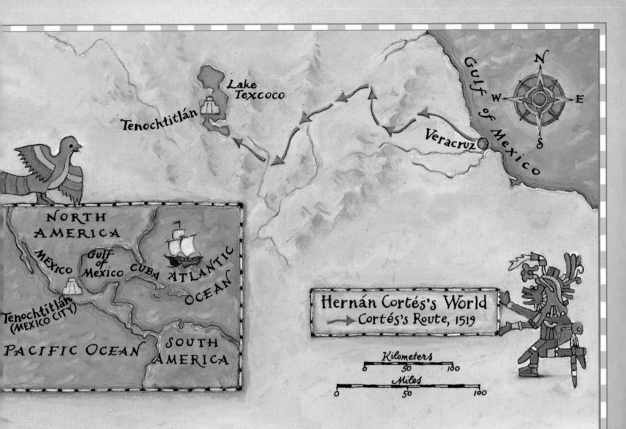

North America, Mexico, Gulf of Mexico, Cuba, Atlantic Ocean, Tenochtitlán (Mexico City), Pacific Ocean, South America

Lake Texcoco, Tenochtitlán, Veracruz, Gulf of Mexico

Hernán Cortés's World
Cortés's Route, 1519

Kilometers
Miles

According to Aztec legend, Quetzalcoatl had left Mexico long ago. He had gone east, promising someday to return. Hearing about Cortés, Moctezuma couldn't help wondering. Cortés was light-skinned. Cortés was bearded. And Cortés had come to Mexico from the east!

Moctezuma decided not to order his soldiers to destroy the Spanish. Instead, he sent ambassadors with gifts for Cortés and his men. Cortés showed the ambassadors how well his men could ride horses and shoot cannons. The ambassadors had never seen either guns or horses. Impressed and terrified, they hurried to tell Moctezuma about the powerful soldiers who had just arrived.

◄ Aztec serpent ornament, one of the gifts sent by Moctezuma to Cortés

THE INVASION OF MEXICO

Soon after the ambassadors left, Cortés ordered his men to march to the Aztec capital, Tenochtitlán (teh–nawch–tee–TLAN). At first, many of his men resisted. These men felt that the whole adventure was doomed, guns or no guns. After all, the Aztecs had thousands of trained soldiers!

Cortés wanted the wealth of Mexico. He ordered his men to march forward into the heart of Moctezuma's empire. To make sure no one turned back, he burned the ships. Now the Spanish had to defeat the Aztecs if they wanted to return home.

Cortés was a crafty leader. He found a Native American woman named Malinche (mah-LIHN-chay) who could speak Spanish.

Cortés and Malinche meet Moctezuma.

With Malinche's help, Cortés talked to many of the other Native American peoples that Moctezuma ruled. Most of these people hated the Aztecs, and many agreed to help Cortés.

Before long, the army stood at the gates of the Aztec capital. The Spanish were awed by the city's size and beauty—and by the thousands of warriors who guarded it. Moctezuma greeted Cortés warmly and offered the Spanish a palace for their visit. Was it a trap?

TRAVELERS' TALES

Aztec temple

Tenochtitlán was built on islands in a lake. To the Spanish, the Aztec capital looked like a city in a fairy tale. One of them later described his first sight of it. "These great towns and temples and buildings rising from the water, all made of stone, seemed like an enchanted vision. Indeed, some of our soldiers asked whether it was not all a dream."

THE NIGHT OF SORROW

Cortés knew the Aztecs might attack at any moment. So he made a bold plan. He took Moctezuma prisoner and ruled Mexico through his captive. Cortés had the Aztecs bring him gold and jewels, pretending that this was the emperor's idea.

The Aztecs knew better. Day by day, their bitterness grew. In June 1520, it burst out into open revolt. Waving spears and shooting arrows, Aztec warriors pushed the Spanish into a small area around the palace.

Aztecs and Spanish in battle

Worried, Cortés sent Moctezuma out to calm the crowd. But the people of Tenochtitlán were no longer willing to listen. They had chosen a new ruler, they explained, one who would not obey the Spanish. The Aztecs pressed forward. In the heat of battle, Moctezuma was struck in the head. Soon afterwards, he died.

Cortés ordered his men to leave the city. The battle grew ever more furious as the Spanish tried to escape. Again and again, the Aztecs attacked. More than half the Spanish and many of the Native Americans with them were killed. That bloody evening would be known as "la noche triste," "the Night of Sorrow."

Moctezuma

Carved head of an Aztec warrior

? IT'S A MYSTERY

WHO KILLED MOCTEZUMA?

It's not certain how the Aztec ruler died. Some sources say that he was killed by his own people. They believe that an angry Aztec hit Moctezuma with a stone or a spear while he was speaking to his subjects. Others say that Cortés had the emperor killed when he saw that Moctezuma could no longer control his people.

FALL OF THE AZTEC EMPIRE

✳

Although the Spanish had been driven from Tenochtitlán, Cortés was in no mood to give up. He gathered new forces and began planning another assault. In the spring of 1521, Cortés returned.

He surrounded the Aztec capital. He did not let people, food, or supplies pass in or out. The Aztec defenders fought back as best they could, but they could not match the Spanish weapons.

◀ An Aztec painting showing the attack of the Spanish and their Native American allies

Nor were there as many Aztecs as there had been. Thousands had already been killed in the fighting. More died in battle every day. Others were dying of European diseases such as smallpox. These diseases had been unknown in Mexico until the arrival of the Spanish.

As the weeks passed, the Aztecs' problems grew worse. Food supplies ran short. Water became undrinkable. Hunger and illness spread through the city. Finally, in August 1521, the Aztecs could fight no longer. Tenochtitlán lay in ruins. The Aztec empire was no more. The Spanish ruled Mexico, which became the **colony** of New Spain.

Aztec Lord of Fire

Aztec mask

ACROSS CULTURES

Shortly after the Spanish conquest of Mexico, some surviving Aztec scholars wrote an account of what had happened. Here they describe the greed of the Spanish when they saw Moctezuma's treasure.

"Next the Spanish went to Moctezuma's storehouse where his personal treasures were kept. The Spaniards grinned like little beasts and patted each other with delight. When they entered the hall of treasures, it was as if they had arrived in Paradise. They searched everywhere and wanted everything; they were slaves to their own greed. All of Moctezuma's possessions were brought out. They seized these treasures as if they were their own, as if this plunder were merely a stroke of good luck."

CHAPTER 3

ROBERT DE LA SALLE

The Spanish were followed by other Europeans in claiming colonies in the New World. The French settled in what is now eastern Canada. It became the colony of New France. French settlers there heard stories of a great river to the west. They hoped this river might finally empty into the Pacific Ocean. Europeans were still looking for a route to Asia.

The first French explorer to search for the river was Robert Cavelier, Sieur de La Salle. La Salle was an adventurous merchant and farmer who came to New France as a young man. In 1669, La Salle headed south of Lake Ontario on a four-year trip in search of the great river.

Robert de La Salle

La Salle's World
→ La Salle's Route, 1679-1682

Lake Superior
CANADA
Lake Huron
Lake Michigan
Lake Ontario
St. Lawrence R.
Montreal
Illinois River
Lake Erie
APPALACHIAN MTS.
ATLANTIC OCEAN
Mississippi River
Gulf of Mexico
Matagorda

N
W   E
S

Kilometers
0   250   500
Miles
0   250   500

◄ French explorers often used Native American birchbark canoes.

He did not find it. The great river, the Mississippi, was in fact many miles to the west. Though La Salle did not get there first, two other Frenchmen did. In 1673, Louis Jolliet and Jacques Marquette came west by canoe from Lake Michigan. Carrying their boats between waterways, they paddled until they reached the Mississippi River. Then they traveled far downstream. Marquette and Jolliet realized that the mighty river drained south into the Gulf of Mexico, not west into the Pacific.

EXPLORING THE GREAT LAKES

La Salle was disappointed not to have been the first European on the Mississippi. But he knew there was still a vast wilderness to be explored. La Salle's next project was to explore the Great Lakes.

To do this, La Salle built the *Griffin*, the first sailing ship on the Great Lakes. He sailed the *Griffin* through Lake Erie, Lake Huron, and Lake Michigan. All along the way, he and his crew traded furs with Native Americans.

La Salle overseeing the launching of the *Griffin*

La Salle and his men on frozen Lake Michigan

After he reached Lake Michigan, La Salle decided to explore the western rivers for himself. Sending the *Griffin* back to New France with a load of furs, he set off on a canoe journey with the rest of the crew. He and his men paddled down the Illinois River to a spot where they built a fort.

La Salle planned to stay and explore further, but his supplies were running low. It was midwinter, and he and his crew had to return to New France in the bitter cold. Luckily, he was a skilled traveler by now. He made it safely back home and returned later with the supplies he needed.

A compass of La Salle's time

AN EMPIRE FOR FRANCE

La Salle dreamed of a French empire that would cover most of North America. The key to this empire, he decided, was the Mississippi River. Whoever controlled the Mississippi could claim the lands for many miles on both sides. Before France could do this, a French explorer needed to travel down the river to its end.

La Salle intended to be that explorer. In early 1682, he led a fleet of canoes down the Mississippi. Within a few weeks, he reached the point where the river flowed into the Gulf of Mexico. Overjoyed, La Salle claimed the whole river—and the land around it—for France.

La Salle claiming Louisiana for France

He called this region "Louisiana" in honor of the French king, Louis XIV. La Salle was eager to help his country. He also hoped that the king would reward him for claiming vast new lands for France. Gold would be nice, but what La Salle really wanted was Louisiana. He hoped that the king would put him in charge of the whole territory.

The Mississippi River and its surrounding valley

TRAVELERS' TALES

La Salle named Louisiana in a ceremony on April 9, 1682. He and his men put up a huge wooden cross on the southernmost tip of land they could find. Then La Salle gave a speech in which he claimed for France all "the seas, harbors, ports, bays, peoples, provinces, cities, towns, villages, mines, minerals, fisheries, streams, and rivers" of the huge river valley.

DEATH IN THE WILDERNESS

✳

As La Salle had hoped, King Louis was delighted with his hard work. The king ordered La Salle back to France and made him governor of Louisiana. La Salle set sail for the Gulf of Mexico with four ships and 400 settlers. His plan was to start a colony near the mouth of the Mississippi.

La Salle believed this colony would make the French "masters of the whole of this continent." Things did not work out as he planned. La Salle got lost on his way back to Louisiana. He landed about 400 miles west of the Mississippi at Matagorda Bay, in what is now Texas.

◄ La Salle showing the king a chart of Louisiana

▼ The cover of La Salle's travel records

La Salle's most important ship on this voyage was called the *Belle*. It sank in Matagorda Bay in January 1686. More than 300 years later, archaeologists found the wreck of the ship at the bottom of the bay. They have been studying it ever since.

THEN & NOW

A dam built to help dig up the *Belle*

From there, things quickly grew worse. Two of the ships sank, taking with them most of the food and fresh water. The settlers began to die of disease and starvation. They pleaded with La Salle to send for help. But he refused to pay much attention to their needs.

Finally, in 1685, two full years after the settlers landed, La Salle led them away from Texas. By then, however, they were simply too angry to listen to him any longer. Some of the settlers seized La Salle, killed him, and left his body in the wilderness.

THE WORLD IN 1700

The arrival of European explorers in the Western Hemisphere was one of the most important events in world history. Europe and the "New World" were brought together for the first time. Plants, animals, and diseases were carried back and forth between the Old World and the Americas. This process is called the **Columbian Exchange**.

For Europeans, this process was mostly good. They got to know American foods like pineapple and chocolate. For the Native Americans, the Columbian Exchange was largely a disaster. They got to know about guns and germs. In their greed for land and gold, Europeans destroyed the great Native American civilizations.

The Columbian Exchange included fur trading.

Millions of Native Americans died from diseases brought to the Western Hemisphere by Europeans. By 1700, the Columbian Exchange was far from complete. However, things had already changed forever on both sides of the Atlantic.

GLOSSARY

caravel a small ship with several three-sided lateen sails

carrack a larger version of the caravel, with both lateen and square sails

colony an area ruled by another country

Columbian Exchange the movement of plants, animals, and diseases between Europe and the Western Hemisphere that resulted from European exploration and colonization

conquistador or "conqueror," a Spanish soldier-explorer of the 1500s

Indies an old name for lands in eastern Asia that were the source of valuable spices

lateen a three-sided sail

logbook or log, a record of a voyage

merchant a trader

mutiny a revolt aboard ship

Spanish map of Tenochtitlán, which was built on islands in a lake
▼

INDEX